Why don't your eyeballs fall out?

and other questions about the HUMAN BODY

Anna Claybourne

WAYLAND
www.waylandbooks.co.uk

First published in Great Britain in 2020
by Wayland

Credits:
Editor: Julia Bird
Design and illustrations: Matt Lilly
Cover Design: Matt Lilly

HB ISBN 978 1 5263 1 1368
PB ISBN 978 1 5263 1 1375

Printed and bound in China

FSC
www.fsc.org

MIX
Paper from
responsible sources
FSC® C104740

Picture credits:

Every effort has been made to clear copyright. Should there
be any inadvertent omission, please apply to the publisher for
rectification.

Science Picture Library: Jacopin/BSIP 17t; SCIMAT 19tr.
Shutterstock: AP/REX 9t; Boonrod 23cr; Ger Bosma Photos
8bl; Christoph Burgstedt 11t; Butterfly Hunter 29b; Colorsport/
REX 20c; crab garden 27cl; Evvika 14tr; Peter Hermes Furian
22b; Happy Stock Photo 12tr; Here 6r; HunterKitty 23br;
Independent Birds 8br; jannoon028 15tr; Nick Kashenko
11cr; Kateryna Kon 12br; LeventeGyori 21b; TY Lim 12cr;
Love Silhouette 12cl; Naeblys 13t; Maks Narodenko 15br; M
Unal Ozmen 17br, 23tr; Patrice6000 24br; Alexander Popatov
7t; Jerome Scholler 27cr; Svetlana Serebryakova 17br;
Shayneppistockphoto 29c; Tatiana Shepeleva 12bc; Solent
News/REX 27b; stockphoto mania 20tr; Sviatlana St 10tr, 11b;
Alfonso de Tomas 18b; Suzanne Tucker 28b; Valentin Volkov
14c; Peter Waters 11b; Christian Weber 6l; Yellow Cat 11cl.

Wayland
An imprint of
Hachette Children's Group
Part of Hodder and Stoughton
Carmelite House
50 Victoria Embankment
London EC4Y 0DZ

An Hachette UK Company
www.hachette.co.uk
www.hachettechildrens.co.uk

Contents

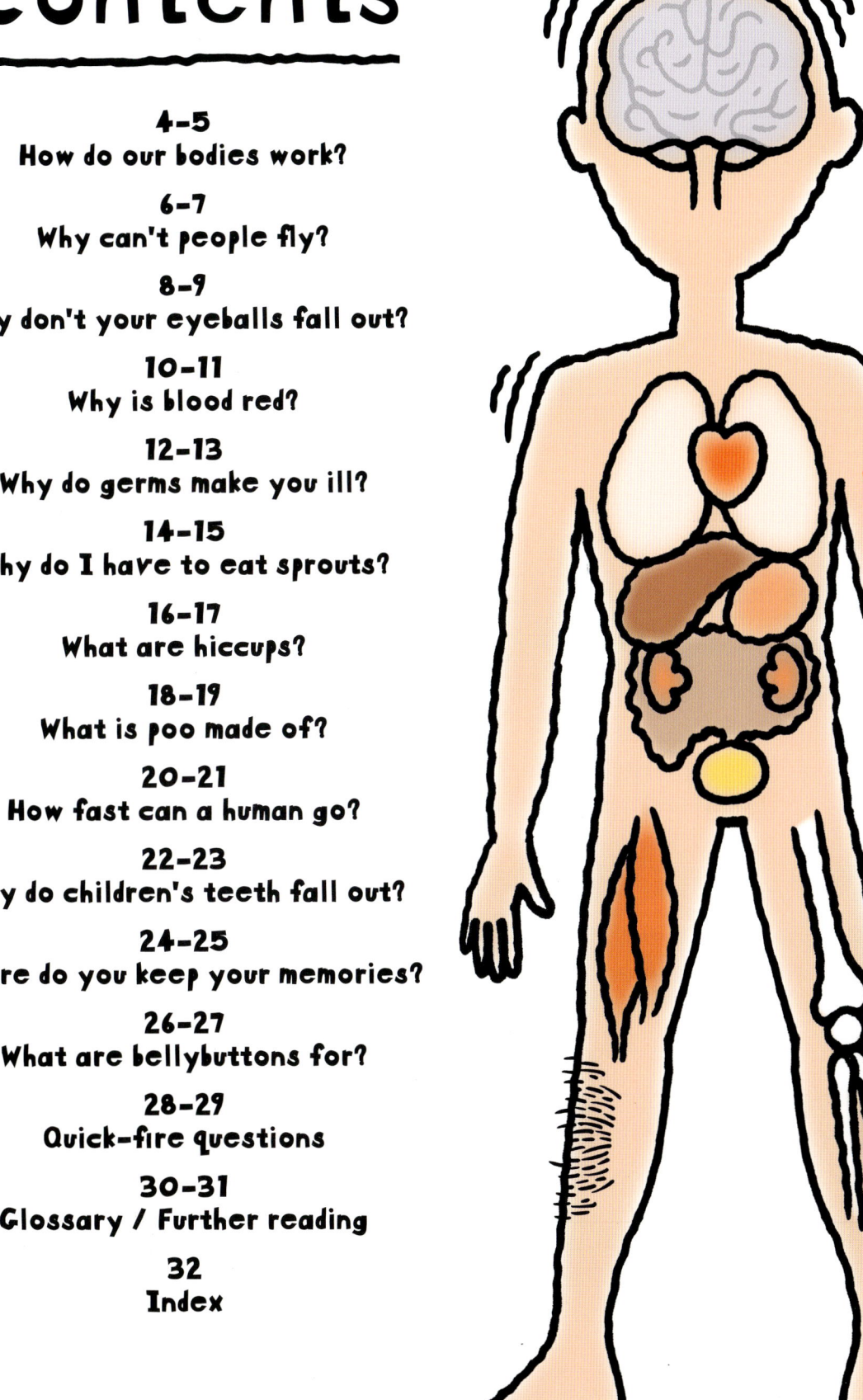

How do our bodies work?

If you're a human, you have a human body. It looks after you and keeps you alive in all kinds of ways...

- It lets you move around
- It takes in food to give you energy
- It breathes in oxygen from the air
- It sees, hears, feels, tastes and smells
- It lets you think, talk to other people, and learn things
- It gets rid of waste... **PLOP!**

How does your body keep on top of all these jobs? It is made up of many different parts. Some are **BIG**, others are very tiny. Each part has its own important job to do.

Cells

All body parts are made of billions and billions of microscopic cells. Cells can split in two to make new cells. This means your body can grow and change, and replace old parts.

I FEEL ALL FLUSHED!

Microscope photo of skin cells

Let's have a closer look inside your body, to see what it's made of and how it works.

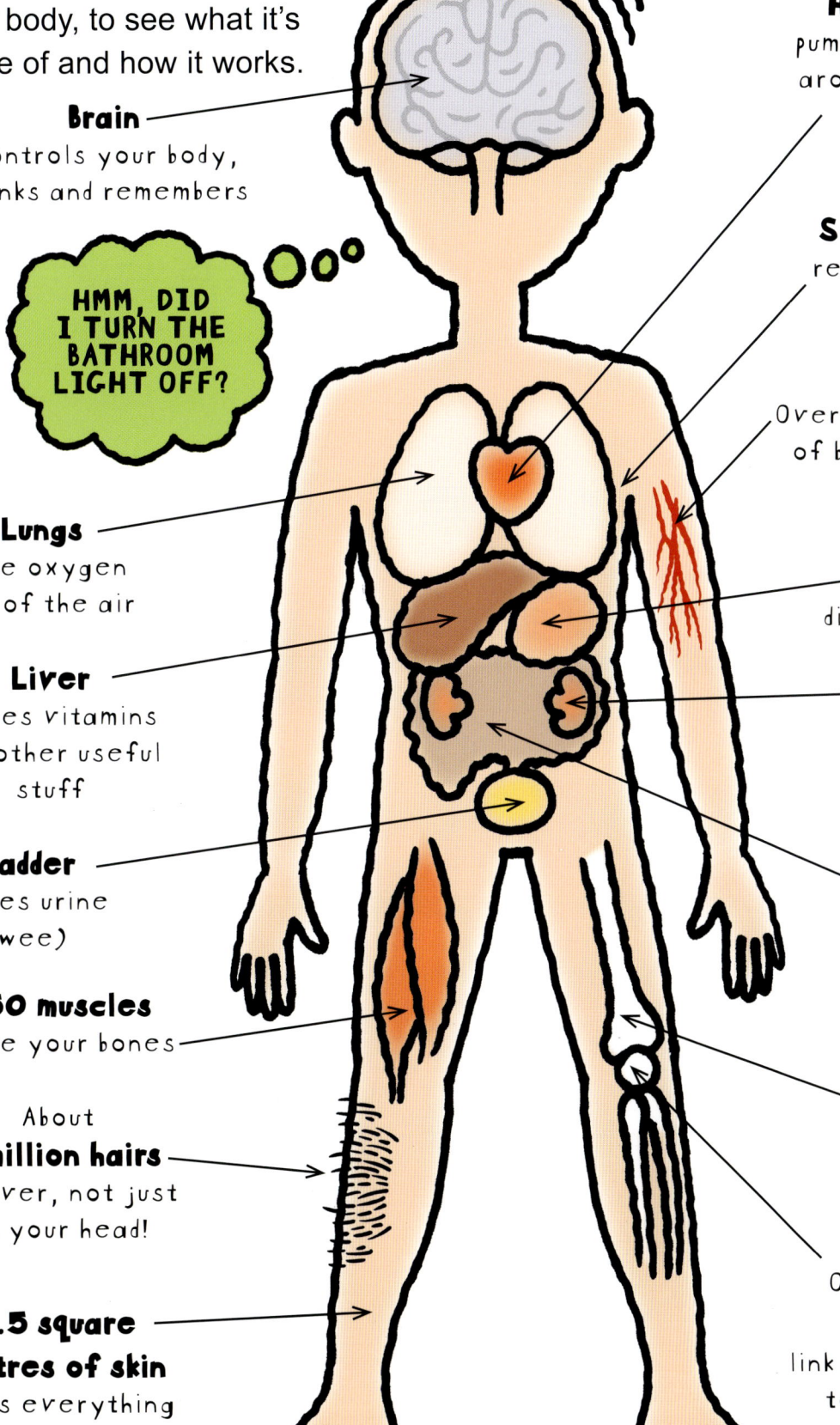

Brain
controls your body, thinks and remembers

HMM, DID I TURN THE BATHROOM LIGHT OFF?

Lungs
take oxygen out of the air

Liver
stores vitamins and other useful stuff

Bladder
stores urine (wee)

650 muscles
move your bones

About
5 million hairs
all over, not just on your head!

1.5 square metres of skin
holds everything in and keeps germs out

Heart
pumps blood around the body

Sweat glands
release sweat!

Over **100,000 km** of blood vessels

Stomach
dissolves food

Kidneys
filter out waste from the blood

Intestines
soak up useful bits from food

At least **206 bones**
hold you up

Over **360 joints**
link your bones to make a skeleton

Why can't people fly?

Since the beginning of time, humans have watched birds flying high in the sky, and wished they could fly too. But flapping your arms just doesn't seem to work (even when you're dressed as a superhero).

The reason birds can fly and we can't is because we have very different bodies. Look at them side by side, and you'll see how.

Long, strong wings

Weaker arms

Squawk!

Powerful chest muscles

Teeny, lightweight legs

Weaker chest muscles

Strong legs for walking

Limbs

Flying birds have smaller legs to reduce their weight, but their 'arm' and 'finger' bones have evolved into long, strong wings.

Humans are built for walking and running, so we have long, strong legs. We use our arms and hands for doing more detailed, fiddly tasks so they are smaller and weaker.

Muscles

Both birds and humans move their arms using large muscles in their chests. But in birds, these muscles are much stronger, so they can flap their huge wings.

Where's the hair?

We humans have hair – great at protecting our heads from sun and rain, but useless for flying. Instead of hair, birds have feathers that spread out to form a wide wing area. When the wings flap, the feathers push air downwards, lifting the bird up.

Soft, wide vane

Albatross feather

Stiff central part

Buzz!

Squeak!

Not all flying creatures have feathers. Insects have thin, light wings made of a clear substance called chitin.

Bats have wings made of thinly stretched skin.

Basically, each animal's body is adapted to help it live in a particular way – and for humans, that's on the ground.

Why don't your eyeballs fall out?

Your eyeballs really are actual balls!

Look at this scan of a human head, and there they are, right in front of the brain.

Eyes

Brain

You don't normally see the whole eyeball, because it sits in a socket in your skull, surrounded by bone, skin and eyelids. But eyeballs can look from side to side, swivel and roll.

So could they actually fall out?

Hold on tight!
Luckily, the answer is **NO**.

Eyeballs are connected to your head by a set of stretchy muscles. They pull the eyeball in different directions, but also stop it from falling out.

Muscle

Muscle

Eyeball

But there are a few people who can pop their eyeballs forwards, so they stick right out, then pop them back in.

Eeeww!

(Don't try this at home.)

But why IS the eye a ball?

There are two reasons.

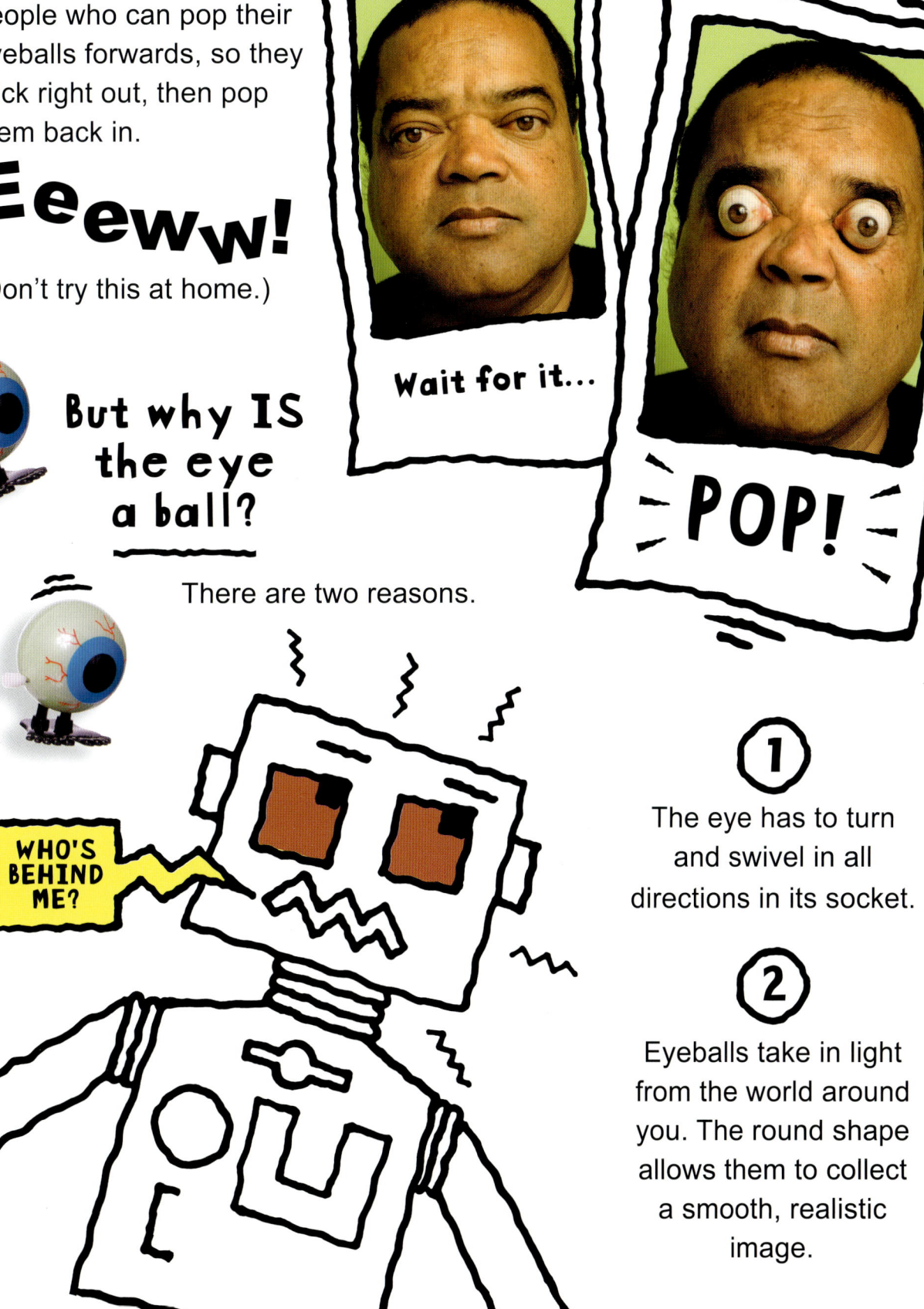

Wait for it...

POP!

WHO'S BEHIND ME?

1

The eye has to turn and swivel in all directions in its socket.

2

Eyeballs take in light from the world around you. The round shape allows them to collect a smooth, realistic image.

Why is blood red?

Bright red blood acts as a useful danger sign. If you see it, it probably means something's gone wrong, and you need to take action.

But how does blood get that colour? It's all to do with its job, delivering useful stuff around your body.

OH NO – WHO'S BLEEDING?!

Delivery!

Your heart pumps blood around your body all the time, through a huge system of blood vessels.

Blood delivers lots of useful things:

Blood vessels

Lungs

Heart

- Nutrients – useful chemicals extracted from food

- Any medicines you've taken

- Hormones – chemicals that control things like your growth and heart rate

- Water, which all your cells need

- And most importantly of all … oxygen gas, which your cells need to work.

The lungs collect oxygen gas from the air when you breathe, and transfer it into your blood.

Blood delivers oxygen to your cells.

Then it returns to the lungs to pick up more oxygen.

What's in blood?

Blood is made of watery plasma, mixed with blood cells. The red blood cells give blood its red colour. They contain iron, which locks onto oxygen. When iron and oxygen combine, they look red.

Red blood cells carry oxygen

Plasma

White blood cells fight germs

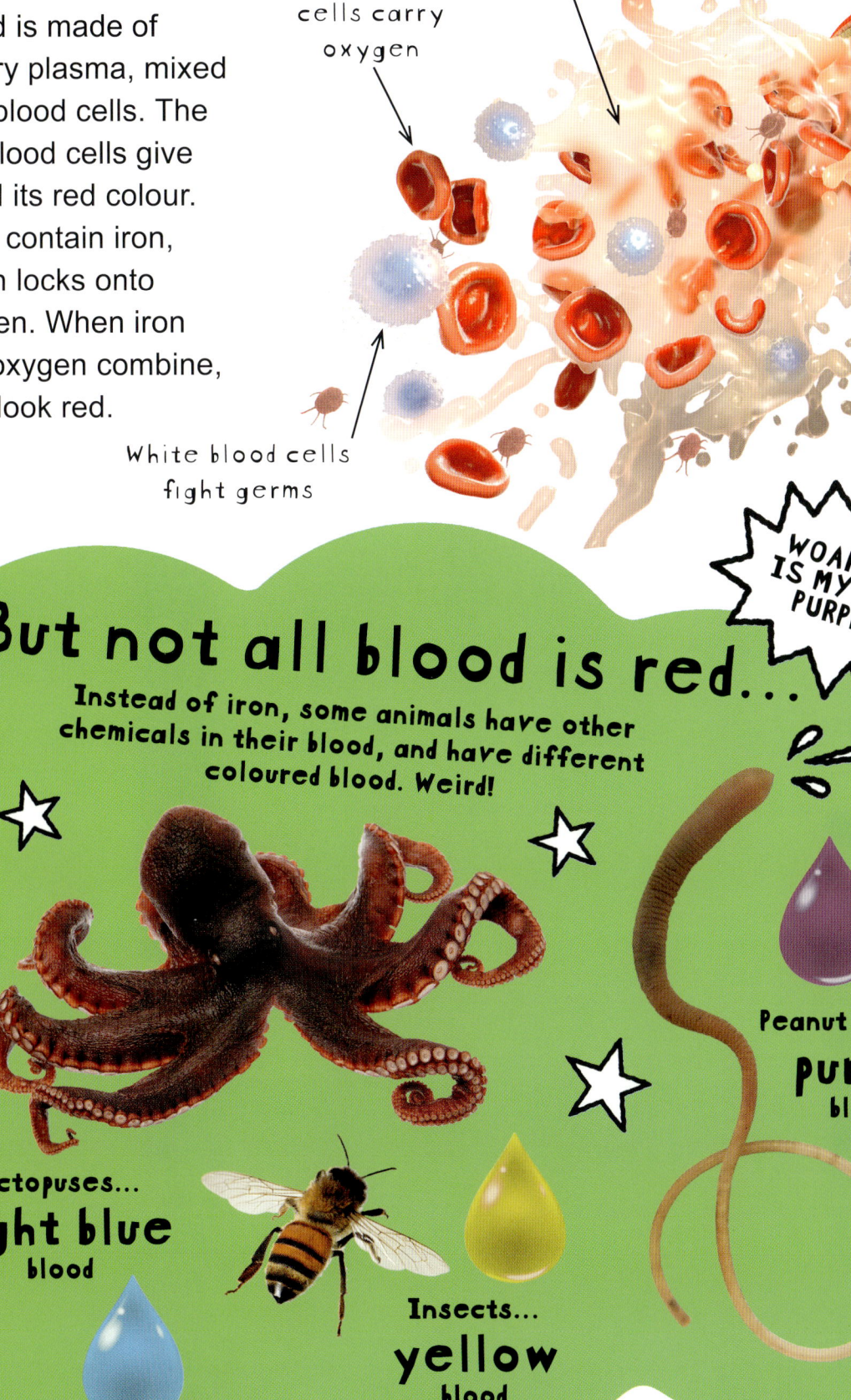

WOAH! WHY IS MY BLOOD PURPLE?!

But not all blood is red...

Instead of iron, some animals have other chemicals in their blood, and have different coloured blood. Weird!

Octopuses...
light blue blood

Insects...
yellow blood

Peanut worms...
purple blood

Why do germs make you ill?

We do all kinds of things to avoid germs. You probably know about most of these, for example…

- Wash your hands after using the toilet... ...And before cooking or eating!
- Don't eat rotten, mouldy food!
- Don't eat undercooked chicken!
- Wash those fruit and vegetables!
- Cover your mouth when you cough and sneeze!

A-choo!

But what's so bad about germs?

Germs are tiny living things, so small you can only see them with a microscope. There are several types of germs, such as bacteria, viruses, fungi and protozoans. These tiny creatures aren't always harmful. But some types can cause illness.

These salmonella bacteria cause food poisoning.

These fungus germs give you athlete's foot!

Germ invasion!

Like all living things, germs need food and a place to live. They get this by invading, or infecting, our bodies. For example, the flu virus gets in through your nose or mouth when you breathe.

Microscopic flu virus

But why do germs make you ill?

There are several ways germs can make you sick...

Some release chemicals that damage cells, giving you a sore throat or headache.

Some take over or kill cells, causing weakness or pain.

Your body may try to kill the germs by heating up, giving you a fever.

Your body also makes germ-fighting cells to attack the germs. That's a good thing, but it uses up your energy, leaving you exhausted.

IT'S NOT OUR FAULT!

Germs don't mean to make you miserable! They're just doing whatever they can to survive, like all living things.

13

Why do I have to eat sprouts?

EAT YOUR GREENS!

We all know that some foods are better for us than others. And most of us are always being told to eat more of the healthy ones!

Here are some of the healthier foods...

Fish

Meat

Bread

...But these aren't always our favourite foods!

Pasta

Sweets

Fruit and vegetables

Many people love eating foods like these. And a lot of people really don't like eating sprouts.

Chocolate

What's that all about?
Surely if some foods are good for our bodies, we should naturally want to eat them, and not all that fast food and junk food?

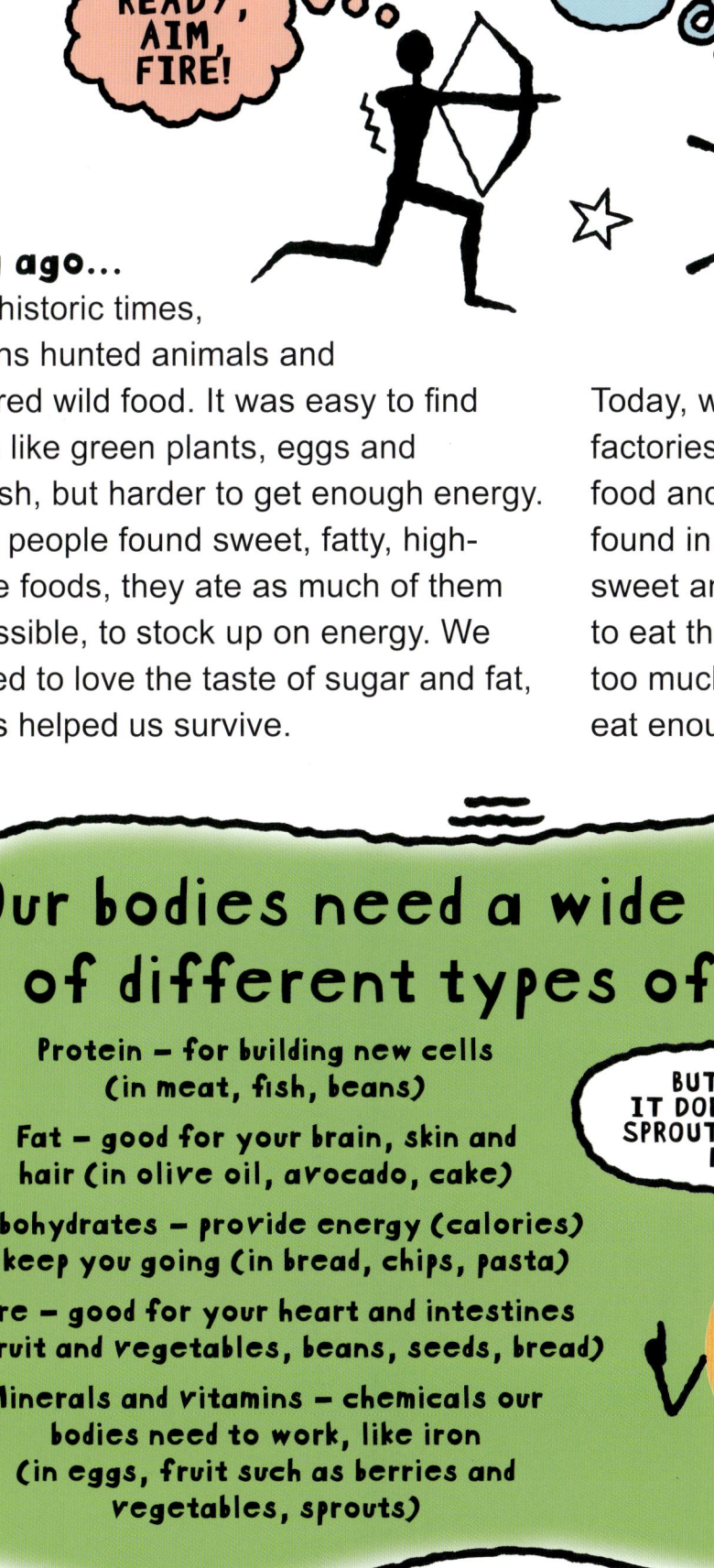

READY, AIM, FIRE!

GULP!!

Long ago…

In prehistoric times, humans hunted animals and gathered wild food. It was easy to find things like green plants, eggs and shellfish, but harder to get enough energy. When people found sweet, fatty, high-calorie foods, they ate as much of them as possible, to stock up on energy. We evolved to love the taste of sugar and fat, as this helped us survive.

Today, we have farms and factories, and high-energy fast food and snacks that aren't found in the wild. We still love sweet and fatty foods and want to eat them – but it's easy to eat too much of them and forget to eat enough of the other stuff.

Our bodies need a wide variety of different types of food.

Protein – for building new cells (in meat, fish, beans)

Fat – good for your brain, skin and hair (in olive oil, avocado, cake)

Carbohydrates – provide energy (calories) to keep you going (in bread, chips, pasta)

Fibre – good for your heart and intestines (in fruit and vegetables, beans, seeds, bread)

Minerals and vitamins – chemicals our bodies need to work, like iron (in eggs, fruit such as berries and vegetables, sprouts)

BUT DON'T PANIC! IT DOESN'T HAVE TO BE SPROUTS, IF YOU REALLY HATE THEM.

What are hiccups?

HIC! HIC! O HIC! o

If you've had hiccups (and most people have) you'll know they can be VERY annoying.

So what are hiccups for?

Well, as far as we can tell, they're completely pointless. They happen when your nervous system gets confused.

Your nervous system

The nervous system is made up of:

The brain

The spinal cord, which carries signals in and out of the brain.

A network of nerves, reaching all over the body.

The nervous system is incredibly important. Its job is to carry signals between your brain and body.

For example...

① You stand on a sharp toy brick.

② The pain signal zooms up the nerves in your foot, leg and spinal cord, to your brain.

③ OUCH! STOOD ON SOMETHING! TAKE ACTION!

④ Your brain sends a signal back, telling you to move your foot.

⑤ QUICK! LIFT UP FOOT.

Mixed-up messages

Now back to those hiccups…

Under your lungs is a big sheet of muscle called the diaphragm. It helps you to breathe by pulling your lungs down, sucking air in.

Phrenic nerve

The phrenic nerve carries signals from the brain to the diaphragm to make it work.

Diaphragm

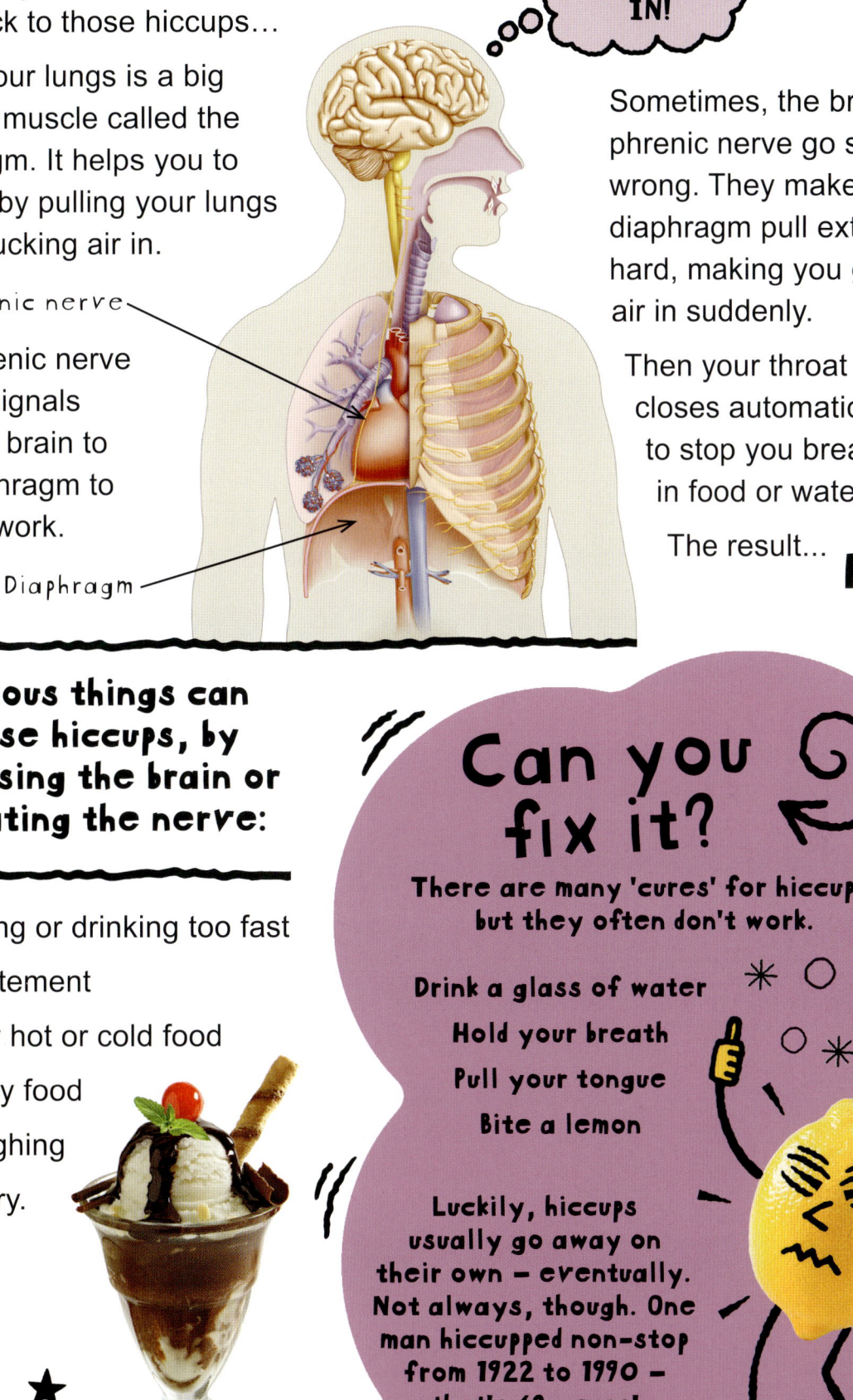

BREATHE IN!

Sometimes, the brain or phrenic nerve go slightly wrong. They make the diaphragm pull extra hard, making you gasp air in suddenly.

Then your throat closes automatically, to stop you breathing in food or water.

The result... **HIC!**

Various things can cause hiccups, by confusing the brain or irritating the nerve:

- Eating or drinking too fast
- Excitement
- Very hot or cold food
- Spicy food
- Laughing
- Worry.

Can you fix it?

There are many 'cures' for hiccups, but they often don't work.

Drink a glass of water

Hold your breath

Pull your tongue

Bite a lemon

Luckily, hiccups usually go away on their own – eventually. Not always, though. One man hiccupped non-stop from 1922 to 1990 – that's 68 years!

What is poo made of?

We all know a poo when we see one.
After all, everyone poos!

But have you ever wondered what poo actually is?

- Why is it brown and squishy?
- Why does it smell so gross?
- And why do we have to poo at all?

The purpose of poo

You poo to remove waste from your body – especially the leftover bits of food that your body can't use, such as fruit pips and vegetable skins. However, poo also contains lots of other stuff.

You can see exactly what in this poo chart!

Poo is coated in a thin layer of slimy mucus, similar to snot. It's made by the intestines to help the poo slide along easily.

Like the rest of your body, about **75%** of a typical poo is water. The water makes the poo soft and squishy, so it can get out of the body easily.

Another **6%** is made of other waste, like dead, broken-down body cells, fat and minerals.

The leftover food waste makes up only around **7%**.

MMM, LUNCH!

And around **12%** is made up of bacteria that live inside your intestines.

Poo is alive!

Your intestines contain billions of bacteria that help to digest food. When the bacteria come out in poo, about half of them are still alive!

SPLOT!

The live bacteria can make you ill if they get into your stomach. This is why poo can be harmful, and you have to flush it away and wash your hands.

Bacteria

Poo through a microscope

Poo Puzzlers

Q: Why is poo brown?

A: The brown colour comes from bilirubin, a chemical made from dead red blood cells.

Q: Why does it smell?

A: The smell mainly comes from the bacteria, and the gases and chemicals they release.

Q: Why is it so gross?

A: We have evolved to find the look and smell of poo disgusting. This makes us avoid it, helping to keep us safe from the germs!

SO DON'T TOUCH IT!!!

How fast can a human go?

A runner waits on the Olympic starting block.
On your marks...
get set...

BANG!

And he's off!

Pushing himself to the absolute limit, he manages to sprint a 100 m distance in less than 10 seconds, reaching a top speed of about 44.5 km/h. And that's about the fastest that any human can run.

Usain Bolt broke the world 100 m record in 2008.

But that's not very fast!

We're used to zooming around in cars and planes at much higher speeds than 44.5 km/h, so it may not seem that fast. But it is very fast for a human runner.

Muscle power

To run fast, we mainly use the muscles in our legs and feet. Like all body cells, muscle cells need oxygen to work.

We breathe oxygen into our lungs, and they pass the oxygen into the blood.

The heart pumps the blood around the body, including to the muscles.

The muscle cells use oxygen to turn fuel from food into energy, so they can move.

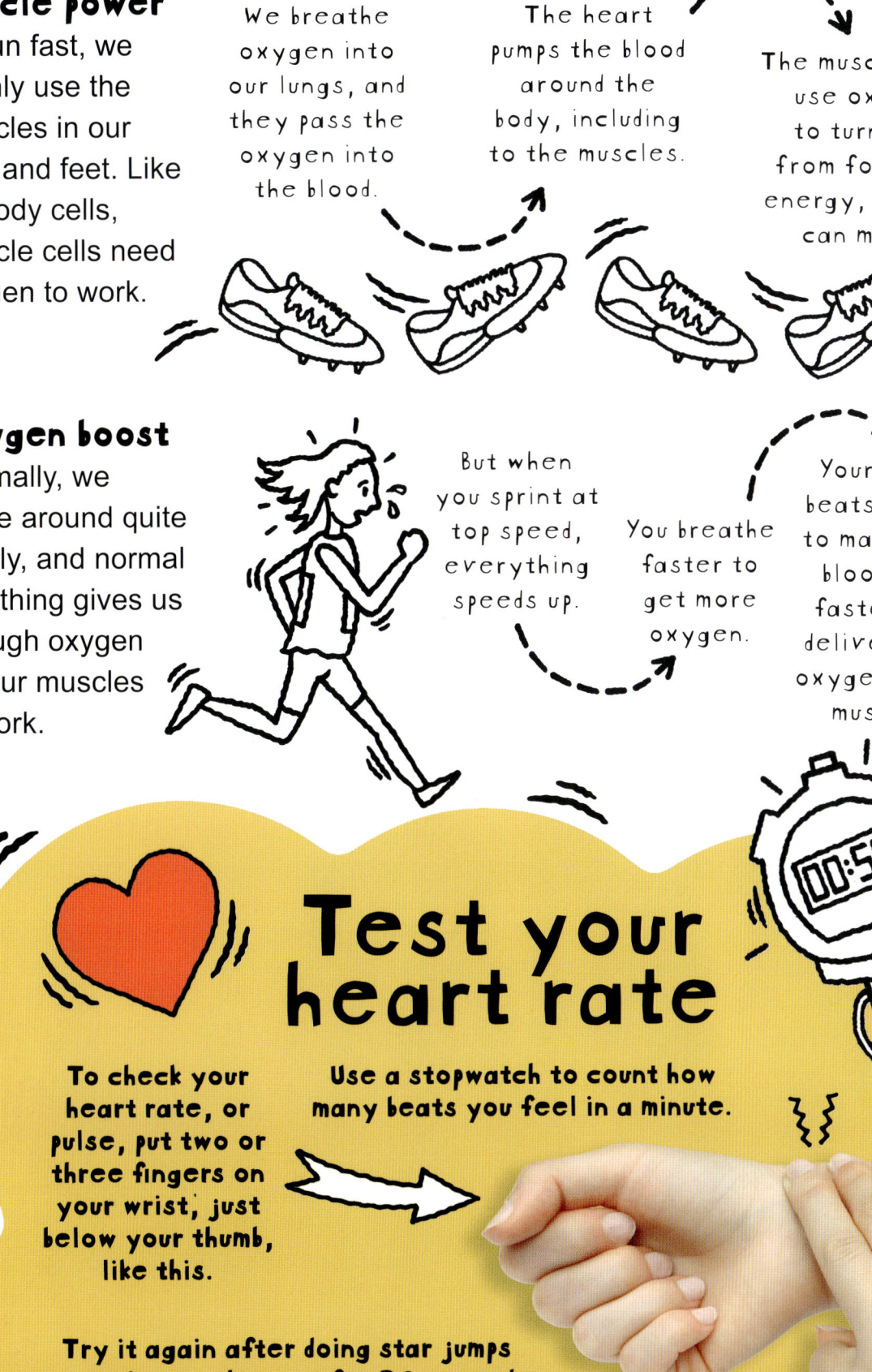

Oxygen boost

Normally, we move around quite slowly, and normal breathing gives us enough oxygen for our muscles to work.

But when you sprint at top speed, everything speeds up.

You breathe faster to get more oxygen.

Your heart beats faster to make your blood flow faster, and deliver more oxygen to the muscles.

Test your heart rate

To check your heart rate, or pulse, put two or three fingers on your wrist, just below your thumb, like this.

Use a stopwatch to count how many beats you feel in a minute.

Try it again after doing star jumps or running on the spot for 30 seconds. How much faster is your pulse?

Why do children's teeth fall out?

If you think about it, it's a bit weird that parts of your body fall off! But we all go through this with our teeth, once we're about five or six years old.

As you get older, your body, including your head and mouth, grow bigger. The bones in your skeleton can grow, but teeth can't just keep growing.

So, you need a smaller set of teeth when you're little...
... and bigger, stronger ones for when you grow up.

The first set are called baby teeth, milk teeth or primary teeth. Most children grow 20 baby teeth.

When you're older, you have a bigger mouth and space for more teeth. Most people have 32 adult teeth by the time they reach their early 20s.

OPEN WIDE!

Incisors

Canines

Milk teeth

Molars

Incisors

Canine teeth

Adult teeth

Molars

Premolars

Dropping out!

A baby tooth starts to wobble when an adult tooth pushes up underneath it.

①

Even when you still have baby teeth, the adult teeth are inside your jaw bones, waiting to come out!

② The baby tooth's root dissolves, so it can fall out more easily.

③ When the adult tooth is ready, it starts to push on the wobbly baby tooth.

④ The adult tooth pushes the baby tooth right out.

POP!

Take care of them!

Once you get your adult teeth, that's it – you won't get any more. So it's important to look after them and keep them clean.

SUGARY DRINKS ARE BAD FOR THE LIKES OF ME!

Animal teeth

Kittens and puppies have milk teeth too, and so do some other animals.

Baby elephants grow milk tusks!

Sharks have many rows of teeth. As the front row wears out, another row moves forward to replace it.

Where do you keep your memories?

You learn and memorise new stuff all the time. Not just facts at school, but all kinds of other things too, like…

- How long to boil the perfect egg
- What new words mean
- How to tie shoelaces
- Your favourite song
- The way to school
- Names and faces.

Where does all that stuff go?

Into your head, of course!

But where exactly do you put it, and how does it stay there? Your brain doesn't contain a computer drive, or a library full of tiny books. In fact, the human brain is more like a big blob of wrinkly-looking, pinkish-grey jelly! But it can store vast amounts of information, sights, sounds, smells, tastes, ideas and memories.

Cortex

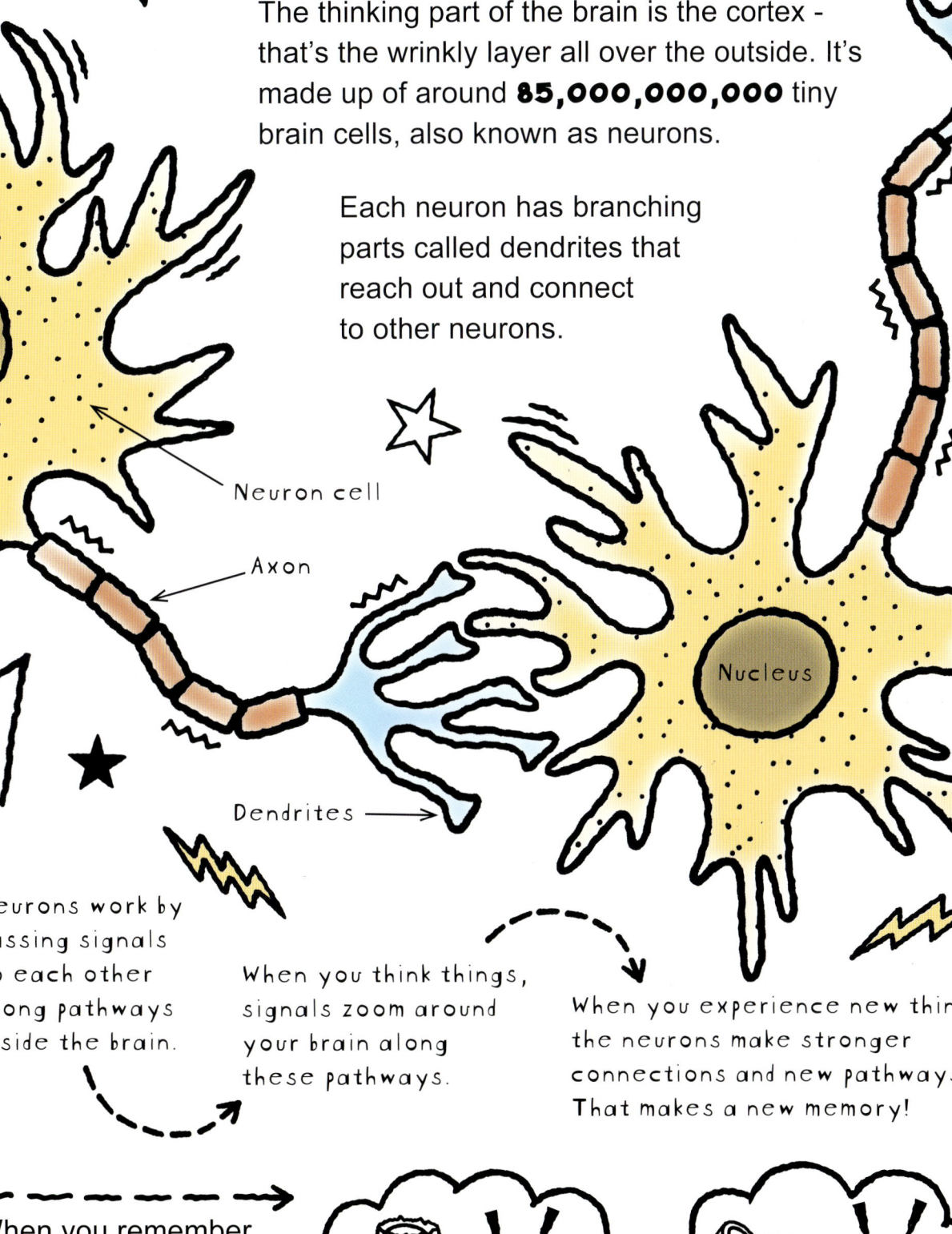

The brain network

The thinking part of the brain is the cortex - that's the wrinkly layer all over the outside. It's made up of around **85,000,000,000** tiny brain cells, also known as neurons.

Each neuron has branching parts called dendrites that reach out and connect to other neurons.

Neuron cell

Axon

Nucleus

Dendrites

Neurons work by passing signals to each other along pathways inside the brain.

When you think things, signals zoom around your brain along these pathways.

When you experience new things, the neurons make stronger connections and new pathways. That makes a new memory!

When you remember the memory, signals zoom along the same pathways again.

BING!

BING!

25

What are bellybuttons for?

You walk around all the time with a pretty pointless body part – your bellybutton! It doesn't lead anywhere or do anything. But it wasn't always useless. In fact, long ago, it used to keep you alive.

Baby button

When a baby is growing inside a woman's body, it can't breathe or eat. It floats inside a closed bag of watery liquid.

Babies still need food and oxygen.

To deliver these, blood flows into the baby from the mother's body, through a tube called the umbilical cord.

Growing baby

Umbilical cord

Amniotic sac (bag)

Amniotic fluid (liquid)

Womb (the organ that holds the growing baby)

The bellybutton, or navel, is the place where the tube enters the baby.

Cutting the cord

After a baby is born, it can start breathing and feeding the normal way, so it doesn't need its umbilical cord any more. The cord is cut, leaving a stump that falls off after a few days…

SNIP!

… and the bellybutton is left behind!

Innie or outie?

Some people's bellybuttons go inwards, while others stick out slightly. Whether you have an 'innie' or an 'outie' depends on how the bellybutton closes up and heals over after birth – but both versions are normal and healthy.

About 80% of people have an innie…

…and 20% have an outie!

Bellybutton fluff

Navel Fluff 1984-1993

Navel Fluff 1994-2000

Navel Fluff 2001-

If you have an innie bellybutton, fluff from your clothes can sometimes collect in it. One man collected his bellybutton fluff in jars for 26 years! He's in *The Guinness Book of World Records* for world's largest bellybutton fluff collection.

Eeeww!

Quick-fire questions

What is your appendix for?

The appendix is a little finger-shaped tube leading off your large intestine. Scientists used to think it was useless. But now they think it probably acts as a store of helpful bacteria.

Appendix

How many cells are there in the human body?

It depends on how big you are, but on average, scientists think the human body has about 37 trillion cells. That's 37 million million, or...

37,000,000,000,000!

Y-A-W-N!

Why are yawns catching?

Yawning can help you to stay awake or alert by giving your brain extra oxygen. When you see someone yawning, you want to yawn too. This may have evolved to help everyone in a group of people to stay alert and avoid danger.

Why do we sleep for so long?

ZZZZZz!

You will spend a third of your life fast asleep – typically about 26 years! When you're asleep, your body heals damage and makes new cells, and your brain sorts out and stores memories. All this takes time, so most people need at least seven hours of sleep a night.

How long does it take food to go through you?

FLUSH!

It's different for different people, and for different food! Usually, it takes between one and three days between eating a meal, and the leftovers from that meal coming out in your poo.

PIECES OF EIGHT?

ACTUALLY, I THINK NINE!

Why can humans talk but animals can't?

Humans are very smart and live in groups, and this has helped us to develop language. Our throats, tongues and teeth have evolved to make many different shapes to form words. Other animals don't have such complex languages, but some, like parrots, can copy the word sounds we make.

Glossary

Appendix A small, finger-like tube connected to the large intestine.

Bacteria Single-celled living things that can sometimes act as germs and cause diseases.

Blood vessels The tubes that carry blood around your body.

Carbohydrates Nutrients that give you energy, found in foods such as pasta and bread.

Cells The tiny building blocks that the human body is made up of.

Diaphragm A powerful muscle under your lungs that pulls down to help you breathe.

Evolve To develop and change over time.

Fever A high body temperature, caused by your body when you are ill to try to kill germs.

Glands Small body parts that release useful substances, such as sweat or hormones.

Hormones Body chemicals that affect the way the body works or grows.

Microscopic So tiny you can only see it through a microscope.

Mucus A slippery-snot-like substance made in some parts of the body.

Nerves Pathways that carry signals between the brain and the rest of the body.

Neurons Nerve cells that make up the nerves and the brain.

Nutrients Useful chemicals in food that give your body what it needs to be healthy.

Oxygen A gas found in the air, which you need to breathe in to make all your cells work.

Plasma A runny yellow liquid that is one of the main ingredients in blood.

Protein Nutrients that help to build and repair your body, found in foods such as meat, cheese and lentils.

Pulse The beating of your heart, which can be felt in blood vessels around the body.

Viruses Very tiny germs that can cause some diseases, such as flu.

Further reading

Websites

www.dkfindout.com/uk/human-body/your-amazing-body/

Information to improve your knowledge of human body systems and more.

kidshealth.org/en/kids/center/htbw-main-page.html?WT.ac=k-nav-htbw-main-page

Facts, videos, activities and quizzes about every part of the body.

www.bbc.com/education/topics/zcyycdm

Information, videos and quizzes about how the human body works

www.fizzicseducation.com.au/category/150-science-experiments/human-body-science/

Human body science experiments and things to make and do.

Books

Mind Webs: Human Body by Anna Claybourne (Wayland, 2014)

Your Brilliant Body series by Paul Mason (Wayland, 2015)

Anatomy: A Cutaway Look Inside the Human Body
by Helene Druvert (Thames & Hudson, 2017)

My Amazing Body Machine
by Robert Winston (DK, 2017)

Human Body: A Monster Activity Book
(Igloo Books, 2019)

Index

A Question of Science titles:

Why can't penguins fly?
and other questions about **ANIMALS**

978 1 4451 1162 7 HB
978 1 4451 1163 4 PB

What are animals?
How can a snake swallow an antelope?
Why don't cats lay eggs?
Why don't caterpillars look
like their parents?
Why can't animals talk to us?
Why can't penguins fly?
Which is the cleverest animal
How do chameleons change colour?
What are camels' humps made of?
How can a cockroach live
without its head?
What happened to the dinosaurs?

Where does lightning come from?
and other questions about **ELECTRICITY**

978 1 4451 1161 0 HB
978 1 4451 1160 3 PB

What is electricity?
How do we make electricity?
Where does electricity come from?
Why do shopping trolleys zap you?
Where does lightning come from?
Why doesn't electricity
leak out of sockets?
Why are electric wires
covered in plastic?
Did people have electricity
in ancient times?
Is an electric eel really electric?
Can electricity bring something
dead back to life?
Will we run out of electricity?
How fast can an electric car go?

Why doesn't the moon fall down?
and other questions about **FORCES**

978 1 4451 1154 2 HB
978 1 4451 1155 9 PB

How do our bodies work?
Why can't people fly?
Why don't your eyeballs fall out?
Why is blood red?
Why do germs make you ill?
Why do I have to eat sprouts?
What are hiccups?
What is poo made of?
How fast can a human go?
Why do children's teeth fall out?
Where do you keep your memories?
What are bellybuttons for?

Why don't your eyeballs fall out?
and other questions about the **HUMAN BODY**

978 1 5263 1136 8 HB
978 1 5263 1137 5 PB

What is a force?
Why doesn't the Moon fall down?
Why does rubbing your hands
together warm them up?
Why don't pond-skaters fall in?
How does a parachute
save your life?
How can a metal boat float?
How can a plane fly upside down?
Why can't people grow
as big as dinosaurs?
Why is falling off a cliff so deadly?
How can a magnet pull something
it's not touching?
How does the tablecloth trick work?
Why can you jump higher
on the Moon?

Why does a mirror show things back to front?
and other questions about **LIGHT**

978 1 4451 1156 6 HB
978 1 4451 1157 3 PB

What is light?
Where does light go when
you switch it off?
Why does a mirror show things
back to front?
Why does the Moon shine?
How can your shadow be taller
than you?
How can binoculars make
things look closer?
Where do the stars go
in the daytime?
What makes things different colours?
Why can't you ever reach a rainbow?
How does light get inside your eyes?
How can an X-ray see through you?
Is an invisibility cloak possible?

Why is ice slippery?
and other questions about **MATERIALS**

978 1 4451 1164 1 HB
978 1 4451 1165 8 PB

What are materials?
Why is ice slippery?
What is everything made of?
How big are atoms and molecules?
Why is air invisible?
Is human hair as strong as steel?
Why does salt disappear in water?
Where do crystals come from?
Why do eggs go solid when
you cook them?
Why does metal feel cold?
What makes the Eiffel Tower grow taller?
Do plastic bags last forever?

How can a plant eat a fly?
and other questions about **PLANTS**

978 1 4451 1158 0 HB
978 1 4451 1159 7 PB

What are plants?
Why don't plants have mouths?
Could we exist without plants?
Why can't plants walk around?
How do cactuses survive
in the desert?
Why do flowers smell nice?
How can a seed grow after
thousands of years?
Do plants have feelings?
Why are trees so big?
Can plants talk to each other?
Could a plant eat a person?
Are there plants on other planets?

Can you hear sounds in space?
and other questions about **SOUND**

978 1 4451 1257 0 HB
978 1 4451 1256 3 PB

What is sound?
How do sounds get inside your ears?
Can you hear sounds in space?
Why can't you see sound waves?
How fast is a supersonic plane?
What was the loudest sound ever?
Why do lions roar but mice squeak?
Where do sound waves go?
Why is it hard to hear underwater?
Can deaf people feel sounds?
Can a sound kill you?
Which animal has the best hearing?

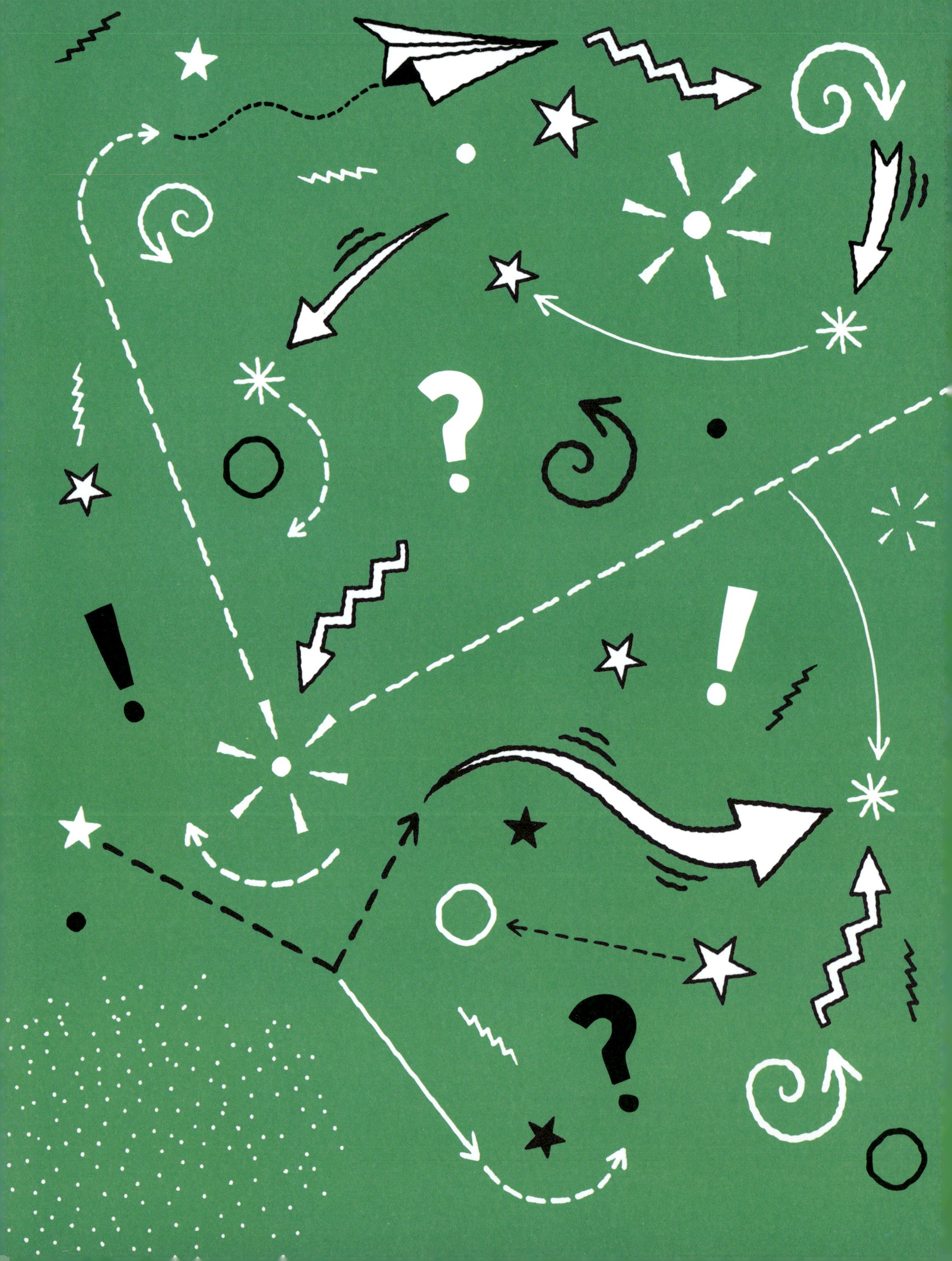